The Poetry of Bliss Carman

Volumes II - Songs From Vagabondia

Co-Authored with Richard Hovey

William Bliss Carman was born in Fredericton, in New Brunswick on April 15th 1861. He was educated at Fredericton Collegiate School before moving to the University of New Brunswick, obtaining his B.A. there in 1881. As is common with so many writers his first published piece was for the University magazine and for Carman that was in 1879.

After several years editing various magazines and periodicals Carman first published a poetry volume in 1893 with Low Tide on Grand Pré. There was no Canadian company prepared to publish and when an American company did so it went bankrupt.

The following year was decidedly better. His partnership with the American poet Richard Hovey had given birth to Songs of Vagabondia. It was an immediate success.

That success prompted the Boston firm, Stone & Kimball, to reissue Low Tide on Grand Pré and to hire Carman as the editor of its literary journal, The Chapbook.

Carman brought out, in 1895, Behind the Arras, a somewhat more serious and philosophical work centered on the premise of a long meditation, using the speaker's house and its many rooms, as a symbol of life and the choices to be made.

In 1896 Carman met Mrs Mary Perry King, who rapidly became patron, adviser and sometime lover. She also became his writing collaborator on two verse dramas.

In 1897 Carman published Ballad of Lost Haven, and in 1898, By the Aurelian Wall, the title poem itself was an elegy to John Keats and the book was a collection of formal elegies.

As the century turned Carman was hard at work on a five-volume set of poetry "Pans Pipes". The excellence of a number of these poems did much to install Carman as the most noted of Canadian Poets and eventually their own Poet Laureate.

In 1912 the final work in the Vagabondia series was published. Richard Hovey had died in 1900 and so this last work was purely Carman's. It has a distinct elegiac tone as if remembering the past works themselves.

On October 28th, 1921 Carman was honored by the newly-formed Canadian Authors' Association where he was crowned Canada's Poet Laureate with a wreath of maple leaves.

William Bliss Carman died of a brain hemorrhage at the age of 68 in New Canaan on the 8th June, 1929.

Index of Contents

VAGABONDIA

Off with the fetters
That chafe and restrain!
Off with the chain!
Here Art and Letters,
Music and wine,
And Myrtle and Wanda,

The winsome witches,
Blithely combine.
Here are true riches,
Here is Golconda,
Here are the Indies,
Here we are free—
Free as the wind is,
Free, as the sea.
Free!

Houp-la!

What have we
To do with the way
Of the Pharisee?
We go or we stay
At our own sweet will;
We think as we say,
And we say or keep still
At our own sweet will,
At our own sweet will.

Here we are free
To be good or bad,
Sane or mad,
Merry or grim
As the mood may be,—
Free as the whim
Of a spook on a spree,—
Free to be oddities,
Not mere commodities,
Stupid and salable,
Wholly available,
Ranged upon shelves;
Each with his puny form
In the same uniform,
Cramped and disabled;
We are not labelled,
We are ourselves.

Here is the real,
Here the ideal;
Laughable hardship
Met and forgot,
Glory of bardship—
World's bloom and world's blot;
The shock and the jostle,
The mock and the push,

But hearts like the throstle
A-joy in the bush;
Wits that would merrily
Laugh away wrong,
Throats that would verily
Melt Hell in Song.

What though the dimes be
Elusive as rhymes be,
And Bessie, with finger
Uplifted, is warning
That breakfast next morning
(A subject she's scorning)
Is mighty uncertain!

What care we? Linger
A moment to kiss—
No time's amiss
To a vagabond's ardor—
Thee finish the larder
And pull down the curtain.

Unless ere the kiss come,
Black Richard or Bliss come,
Or Tom with a flagon,
Or Karl with a jag on—
Then up and after
The joy of the night
With the hounds of laughter
To follow the flight
Of the fox-foot hours
That double and run
Through brakes and bowers
Of folly and fun.

With the comrade heart
For a moment's play,
And the comrade heart
For a heavier day,
And the comrade heart
Forever and aye.

For the joy of wine
Is not for long;
And the joy of song
Is a dream of shine;
But the comrade heart
Shall outlast art

And a woman's love
The fame thereof.

But wine for a sign
Of the love we bring!
And song for an oath
That Love is king!
And both, and both
For his worshipping!

Then up and away
Till the break of day,
With a heart that's merry,
And a Tom-and-Jerry,
And a derry-down-derry—
What's that you say.
You highly respectable
Buyers and sellers?
We should be decenter?
Not as we please inter
Custom, frugality,
Use and morality
In the delectable
Depths of wine-cellars?

Midnights of revel,
And noondays of song!
Is it so wrong?
Go to the Devil!

I tell you that we,
While you are smirking
And lying and shirking
life's duty of duties,
Honest sincerity,
We are in verity
Free!
Free to rejoice
In blisses and beauties!
Free as the voice
Of the wind as it passes!
Free as the bird
In the weft of the grasses!
Free as the word
Of the sun to the sea—
Free!

A WAIF

Do you know what it is to be vagrant born?
A waif is only a waif. And so,
For another idle hour I sit,
In large content while the fire burns low.

I gossip here to my crony heart
Of the day just over, and count it one
Of the royal elemental days,
Though its dreams were few and its deeds were none.

Outside, the winter; inside, the warmth
And a sweet oblivion of turmoil. Why?
All for a gentle girlish hand
With its warm and lingering good-bye.

THE JOYS OF THE ROAD

Now the joys of the road are chiefly these:
A crimson touch on the hard-wood trees;

A vagrant's morning wide and blue,
In early fall when the wind walks, too;

A shadowy highway cool and brown,
Alluring up and enticing down

From rippled water to dappled swamp,
From purple glory to scarlet pomp;

The outward eye, the quiet will,
And the striding heart from hill to hill;

The tempter apple over the fence;
The cobweb bloom on the yellow quince;

The palish asters along the wood, —
A lyric touch of the solitude;

An open hand, an easy shoe.
And a hope to make the day go through, —

Another to sleep with, and a third
To wake me up at the voice of a bird;

The resonant far-listening morn,
And the hoarse whisper of the corn;

The crickets mourning their comrades lost,
In the night's retreat from the gathering frost;

(Or is it their slogan, plaintive and shrill,
As they beat on their corselets, valiant still?)

A hunger fit for the kings of the sea,
And a loaf of bread for Dickon and me;

A thirst like that of the Thirsty Sword,
And a jug of cider on the board;

An idle noon, a bubbling spring,
The sea in the pine-tops murmuring;

A scrap of gossip at the ferry;
A comrade neither glum nor merry,

Asking nothing, revealing naught,
But minting his words from a fund of thought,

A keeper of silence eloquent,
Needy, yet royally well content,

Of the mettled breed, yet abhorring strife,
And full of the mellow juice of life;

A taster of wine, with an eye for a maid,
Never too bold, and never afraid,

Never heart-whole, never heart-sick,
(These are the things I worship in Dick)

No fidget and no reformer, just
A calm observer of ought and must,

A lover of books, but a reader of man,
No cynic and no charlatan,

Who never defers and never demands,
But, smiling, takes the world in his hands,—

Seeing it good as when God first saw
And gave it the weight of his will for law.

And O the joy that is never won,
But follows and follows the journeying sun,

By marsh and tide, by meadow and stream,
A will-o'-the-wind, a light-o'-dream,

Delusion afar, delight anear,
From morrow to morrow, from year to year,

A jack-o'-lantern, a fairy fire,
A dare, a bliss, and a desire!

The racy smell of the forest loam,
When the stealthy, sad-heart leaves go home;

(O leaves, O leaves, I am one with you,
Of the mould and the sun and the wind and the dew!)

The broad gold wake of the afternoon;
The silent fleck of the cold new moon;

The sound of the hollow sea's release
From stormy tumult to starry peace;

With only another league to wend;
And two brown arms at the journey's end!

These are the joys of the open road—
For him who travels without a load.

EVENING ON THE POTOMAC

The fervid breath of our flushed Southern May
Is sweet upon the city's throat and lips,
As a lover's whose tired arm slips
Listlessly over the shoulder of a queen.

Far away
The river melts in the unseen.
Oh, beautiful Girl-City, how she dips
Her feet in the stream
With a touch that is half a kiss and half a dream!
Her face is very fair,
With flowers for smiles and sunlight in her hair.

My westland flower-town, how serene she is!
Here on this hill from which I look at her,
All is still as if a worshipper
Left at some shrine his offering.

Soft winds kiss
My cheek with a slow lingering.
A luring whisper where the laurels stir
Wiles my heart back to woodland-ward again.

But lo,
Across the sky the sunset couriers run,
And I remain
To watch the imperial pageant of the Sun
Mock me, an impotent Cortez here below,
With splendors of its vaster Mexico.

O Eldorado of the templed clouds!
O golden city of the western sky!
Not like the Spaniard would I storm thy gates;
Not like the babe stretch chubby hands and cry

To have thee for a toy; but far from crowds,
Like my Faun brother in the ferny glen,
Peer from the wood's edge while thy glory waits,
And in the darkening thickets plunge again.

SPRING SONG

Make me over, mother April,
When the sap begins to stir!
When thy flowery hand delivers
All the mountain-prisoned rivers,
And thy great heart beats and quivers,
To revive the days that were,
Make me over, mother April,
When the sap begins to stir!

Take my dust and all my dreaming,
Count my heart-beats one by one,
Send them where the winters perish;
Then some golden noon recherish
And restore them in the sun,
Flower and scent and dust and dreaming,
With their heart-beats every one!

Set me in the urge and tide-drift
Of the streaming hosts a-wing!
Breast of scarlet, throat of yellow,
Raucous challenge, wooings mellow—
Every migrant is my fellow,
Making northward with the spring.
Loose me in the urge and tide-drift
Of the streaming hosts a-wing!

Shrilling pipe or fluting whistle,
In the valleys come again;
Fife of frog and call of tree-toad,
All my brothers, five or three-toed,
With their revel no more vetoed,
Making music in the rain;
Shrilling pipe or fluting whistle,
In the valleys come again.

Make me of thy seed to-morrow,
When the sap begins to stir!
Tawny light-foot, sleepy bruin,
Bright-eyes in the orchard ruin,
Gnarl the good life goes askew in,
Whiskey-jack, or tanager,—
Make me anything to-morrow,
When the sap begins to stir!

Make me even (How do I know?)
Like my friend the gargoyle there;
It may be the heart within him
Swells that doltish hands should pin him
Fixed forever in mid-air.
Make me even sport for swallows,
Like the soaring gargoyle there!

Give me the old clue to follow,
Through the labyrinth of night!
Clod of clay with heart of fire,
Things that burrow and aspire,
With the vanishing desire,
For the perishing delight,—
Only the old clue to follow,
Through the labyrinth of night!

Make me over, mother April,
When the sap begins to stir!
Fashion me from swamp or meadow,
Garden plot or ferny shadow,

Hyacinth or humble burr!
Make me over, mother April,
When the sap begins to stir!

Let me hear the far, low summons,
When the silver winds return;
Rills that run and streams that stammer,
Goldenwing with his loud hammer,
Icy brooks that brawl and clamor,
Where the Indian willows burn;
Let me hearken to the calling,
When the silver winds return,

Till recurring and recurring,
Long since wandered and come back,
Like a whim of Grieg's or Gounod's,
This same self, bird, bud, or Bluenose,
Some day I may capture (Who knows?)
Just the one last joy I lack,
Waking to the far new summons,
When the old spring winds come back.

For I have no choice of being,
When the sap begins to climb,—
Strong insistence, sweet intrusion,
Vasts and verges of illusion,—
So I win, to time's confusion,
The one perfect pearl of time,
Joy and joy and joy forever,
Till the sap forgets to climb!

Make me over in the morning
From the rag-bag of the world!
Scraps of dream and duds of daring,
Home-brought stuff from far sea-faring,
Faded colors once so flaring,
Shreds of banners long since furled!
Hues of ash and glints of glory,
In the rag-bag of the world!

Let me taste the old immortal
Indolence of life once more;
Not recalling nor foreseeing,
Let the great slow joys of being
Well my heart through as of yore!
Let me taste the old immortal
Indolence of life once more!

Give me the old drink for rapture,
The delirium to drain,
All my fellows drank in plenty
At the Three Score Inns and Twenty
From the mountains to the main!
Give me the old drink for rapture,
The delirium to drain!

Only make me over, April,
When the sap begins to stir!
Make me man or make me woman,
Make me oaf or ape or human,
Cup of flower or cone of fir;
Make me anything but neuter
When the sap begins to stir!

THE FAUN. A FRAGMENT

I will go out to grass with that old King,
For I am weary of clothes and cooks.
I long to lie along the banks of brooks,
And watch the boughs above me sway and swing.
Come, I will pluck off custom's livery,
Nor longer be a lackey to old Time.
Time shall serve me, and at my feet shall fling
The spoil of listless minutes. I shall climb
The wild trees for my food, and run
Through dale and upland as a fox runs free,
Laugh for cool joy and sleep i' the warm sun,
And men will call me mad, like that old King.

For I am woodland-natured, and have made
Dryads my bedfellows,
And I have played
With the sleek Naiads in the splash of pools
And made a mock of gowned and trousered fools.
Helen, none knows
Better than thou how like a Faun I strayed.
And I am half Faun now, and my heart goes
Out to the forest and the crack of twigs,
The drip of wet leaves and the low soft laughter
Of brooks that chuckle o'er old mossy jests
And say them over to themselves, the nests
Of squirrels and the holes the chipmunk digs,
Where through the branches the slant rays
Dapple with sunlight the leaf-matted ground,

And the wind comes with blown vesture rustling after,
And through the woven lattice of crisp sound
A bird's song lightens like a maiden's face.

O wildwood Helen, let them strive and fret,
Those goggled men with their dissecting-knives!

Let them in charnel-houses pass their lives
And seek in death life's secret! And let
Those hard-faced worldlings prematurely old
Gnaw their thin lips with vain desire to get
Portia's fair fame or Lesbia's carcanet,
Or crown of Caesar or Catullus,
Apicius' lampreys or Crassus' gold!
For these consider many things—but yet
By land nor sea
They shall not find the way to Arcady,
The old home of the awful heart-dear Mother,
Whereto child-dreams and long rememberings lull us,
Far from the cares that overlay and smother
The memories of old woodland out-door mirth
In the dim first life-burst centuries ago,
The sense of the freedom and nearness of Earth—
Nay, this they shall not know;
For who goes thither,
Leaves all the cark and clutch of his soul behind,
The doves defiled and the serpents shrined,
The hates that wax and the hopes that wither;
Nor does he journey, seeking where it be,
But wakes and finds himself in Arcady.

Hist! there's a stir in the brush.
Was it a face through the leaves?
Back of the laurels a skurry and rush
Hillward, then silence except for the thrush
That throws one song from the dark of the bush
And is gone; and I plunge in the wood, and the swift soul cleaves
Through the swirl and the flow of the leaves,
As a swimmer stands with his white limbs bare to the sun
For the space that a breath is held, and drops in the sea;
And the undulant woodland folds round me, intimate, fluctuant, free,
Like the clasp and the cling of waters, and the reach and the effort is done,—
There is only the glory of living, exultant to be.

O goodly damp smell of the ground!
O rough sweet bark of the trees!
O clear sharp cracklings of sound!
O life that's a-thrill and a-bound

With the vigor of boyhood and morning, and the noontide's rapture of ease!
Was there ever a weary heart in the world?
A lag in the body's urge or a flag of the spirit's wings?
Did a man's heart ever break
For a lost hope's sake?
For here there is lilt in the quiet and calm in the quiver of things.
Ay, this old oak, gray-grown and knurled,
Solemn and sturdy and big,
Is as young of heart, as alert and elate in his rest,
As the nuthatch there that clings to the tip of the twig
And scolds at the wind that it buffets too rudely its nest.

Oh, what is it breathes in the air?
Oh, what is it touches my cheek?
There's a sense of a presence that lurks in the branches.
But where?
Is it far, is it far to seek?

A ROVER'S SONG

Snowdrift of the mountains,
Spindrift of the sea,
We who down the border
Rove from gloom to glee,—

Snowdrift of the mountains,
Spindrift of the sea,
There be no such gypsies
Over earth as we.

Snowdrift of the mountains,
Spindrift of the sea,
Let us part the treasure
Of the world in three.

Snowdrift of the mountains,
Spindrift of the sea,
You shall keep your kingdoms;
Joscelyn for me!

DOWN THE SONGO

I.

Floating!
Floating—and all the stillness waits
And listens at the ivory gates,
Full of a dim uncertain presage
Of some strange, undelivered message.
There is no sound save from the bush
The alto of the shy wood-thrush,
And ever and anon the dip
Of a lazy oar.

The rhythmic drowsiness keeps time
To hazy subtleties of rhyme
That seem to slip
Through the lulled soul to seek the sleepy shore.
The idle clouds go floating by;
Above us sky, beneath us sky;
The sun shines on us as we lie
Floating.

It is a dream.
It is a dream, my love; see how
The ripples quiver at the prow,
And all the long reflections shake
Unsteadily beneath the lake.
The mists about the uplands show
Dim violet towers that come and go.
Phantasmagoric palaces
Rise trembling there,
As though one breath of waking weather
Would crash their airy walls together
With sudden stress,
While silent detonations shook the air—
Vast fabrics toppling to the ground
And vanishing without a sound.
Ah, love, these are not what we deem;
It is a dream.

II.

Let us dream on, then,——dream and die
Ere the dream pass.
Let us for once, like idle flowers,
Let slip the unregarded hours,
Like the wise flowers that lie
Unfretted by a feeble thought,
Future and past alike forgot,
Drinking the dew contentedly

In the cool grass.

III.

Look yonder where the clouds float; could we glide
As they, across the sky's blue shoreless tide,
What better were it than to dream
Across yon lake and into this still stream?

IV.

Trees and a glimpse of sky!
And the slow river, quiet as a pool!
And thou and I—and thou and I—
Kiss me! How soft the air is and how cool!

THE WANDER-LOVERS

Down the world with Marna!
That's the life for me!
Wandering with the wandering wind,
Vagabond and unconfined!
Roving with the roving rain
Its unboundaried domain!
Kith and kin of wander-kind,
Children of the sea!

Petrels of the sea-drift!
Swallows of the lea!
Arabs of the whole wide girth
Of the wind-encircled earth!
In all climes we pitch our tents,
Cronies of the elements,
With the secret lords of birth
Intimate and free.

All the seaboard knows us
From Fundy to the Keys;
Every bend and every creek
Of abundant Chesapeake;
Ardise hills and Newport coves
And the far-off orange groves,
Where Floridian oceans break,
Tropic tiger seas.

Down the world with Marna,
Tarrying there and here!
Just as much at home in Spain
As in Tangier or Touraine!
Shakespeare's Avon knows us well,
And the crags of Neufchâtel;
And the ancient Nile is fain
Of our coming near.

Down the world with Marna,
Daughter of the air!
Marna of the subtle grace,
And the vision in her face!
Moving in the measures trod
By the angels before God!
With her sky-blue eyes amaze
And her sea-blue hair!

Marna with the trees' life
In her veins a-stir!
Marna of the aspen heart
Where the sudden quivers start!
Quick-responsive, subtle, wild!
Artless as an artless child,
Spite of all her reach of art!
Oh, to roam with her!

Marna with the wind's will,
Daughter of the sea!
Marna of the quick disdain,
Starting at the dream of stain!
At a smile with love aglow,
At a frown a statued woe,
Standing pinnacled in pain
Till a kiss sets free!

Down the world with Marna,
Daughter of the fire!
Marna of the deathless hope,
Still alert to win new scope
Where the wings of life may spread
For a flight unhazarded!
Dreaming of the speech to cope
With the heart's desire!

Marna of the far quest
After the divine!

Striving ever for some goal
Past the blunder-god's control!
Dreaming of potential years
When no day shall dawn in fears!
That's the Marna of my soul,
Wander-bride of mine!

DISCOVERY

When the bugler morn shall wind his horn,
And we wake to the wild to be,
Shall we open our eyes on the selfsame skies
And stare at the selfsame sea?
O new, new day! though you bring no stay
To the strain of the sameness grim,
You are new, new, new—new through and through,
And strange as a lawless dream.

Will the driftwood float by the lonely boat
And our prisoner hearts unbar,
As it tells of the strand of an unseen land
That lies not far, not far?
O new, new hope! O sweep and scope
Of the glad, unlying sea!
You are new, new, new—with the promise true
Of the dreamland isles to be.

Will the land-birds fly across the sky,
Though the land is not to see?
Have they dipped and passed in the sea-line vast?
Have we left the land a-lee?
O new despair! I though the hopeless air
Grow foul with the calm and grieves,
You are new, new, new—and we cleave to you
As a soul to its freedom cleaves.

Does the falling night hide fiends to fight
And phantoms to affray?
What demons lurk in the grisly mirk,
As the night-watch waits for day?
O strange new gloom! we await the doom,
And what doom none may deem;
But it's new, new, new—and we'll sail it through,
While the mocking sea-gulls scream.

A light, a light, in the dead of night,

That lifts and sinks in the waves!
What folk are they who have kindled its ray,—
Men or the ghouls of graves?
O new, new fear! near, near and near,
And you bear us weal or woe!
But you're new, new, new—so a cheer for you!
And onward—friend or foe!

Shall the lookout call from the foretop tall,
"Land, land!" with a maddened scream,
And the crew in glee from the taffrail see
Where the island palm-trees dream?
New heart, new eyes! For the morning skies
Are a-chant with their green and gold!
New, new, new, new—new through and through!
New, new till the dawn is old!

A MORE ANCIENT MARINER

The swarthy bee is a buccaneer,
A burly velveted rover,
Who loves the booming wind in his ear
As he sails the seas of clover.

A waif of the goblin pirate crew,
With not a soul to deplore him,
He steers for the open verge of blue
With the filmy world before him.

His flimsy sails abroad on the wind
Are shivered with fairy thunder;
On a line that sings to the light of his wings
He makes for the lands of wonder.

He harries the ports of the Hollyhocks,
And levies on poor Sweetbrier;
He drinks the whitest wine of Phlox,
And the Rose is his desire.

He hangs in the Willows a night and a day;
He rifles the Buckwheat patches;
Then battens his store of pelf galore
Under the tautest hatches.

He woos the Poppy and weds the Peach,
Inveigles Daffodilly,

And then like a tramp abandons each
For the gorgeous Canada Lily.

There's not a soul in the garden world
But wishes the day were shorter,
When Mariner B. puts out to sea
With the wind in the proper quarter.

Or, so they say! But I have my doubts;
For the flowers are only human,
And the valor and gold of a vagrant bold
Were always dear to woman.

He dares to boast, along the coast,
The beauty of Highland Heather,—
How he and she, with night on the sea,
Lay out on the hills together.

He pilfers from every port of the wind,
From April to golden autumn;
But the thieving ways of his mortal days
Are those his mother taught him.

His morals are mixed, but his will is fixed;
He prospers after his kind,
And follows an instinct, compass-sure,
The philosophers call blind.

And that is why, when he comes to die,
He'll have an easier sentence
Than some one I know who thinks just so,
And then leaves room for repentance.

He never could box the compass round;
He doesn't know port from starboard;
But he knows the gates of the Sundown Straits,
Where the choicest goods are harbored.

He never could see the Rule of Three,
But he knows a rule of thumb
Better than Euclid's, better than yours,
Or the teachers' yet to come.

He knows the smell of the hydromel
As if two and two were five;
And hides it away for a year and a day
In his own hexagonal hive.

Out in the day, hap-hazard, alone,
Booms the old vagrant hummer,
With only his whim to pilot him
Through the splendid vast of summer.

He steers and steers on the slant of the gale,
Like the fiend or Vanderdecken;
And there's never an unknown course to sail
But his crazy log can reckon.

He drones along with his rough sea-song
And the throat of a salty tar,
This devil-may-care, till he makes his lair
By the light of a yellow star.

He looks like a gentleman, lives like a lord,
And works like a Trojan hero;
Then loafs all winter upon his hoard,
With the mercury at zero.

A SONG BY THE SHORE

"Lose and love" is love's first art;
So it was with thee and me,
For I first beheld thy heart
On the night I last saw thee.
Pine-woods and mysteries!
Sea-sands and sorrows!
Hearts fluttered by a breeze
That bodes dark morrows, morrows,—
Bodes dark morrows!

Moonlight in sweet overflow
Poured upon the earth and sea!
Lovelight with intenser glow
In the deeps of thee and me!
Clasped hands and silences!
Hearts faint and throbbing!
The weak wind sighing in the trees!
The strong surf sobbing, sobbing,—
The strong surf sobbing!

A HILL SONG

Hills where once my love and I
Let the hours go laughing by!
All your woods and dales are sad,—
You have lost your Oread.
Falling leaves! Silent woodlands!
Half your loveliness is fled.
Golden-rod, wither now!
Winter winds, come hither now!
All the summer joy is dead.

There's a sense of something gone
In the grass I linger on.
There's an under-voice that grieves
In the rustling of the leaves.
Pine-clad peaks! Rushing waters!
Glens where we were once so glad!
There's a light passed from you,
There's a joy outcast from you,—
You have lost your Oread.

AT SEA

As a brave man faces the foe,
Alone against hundreds, and sees Death grin in his teeth,
But, shutting his lips, fights on to the end
Without speech, without hope, without flinching,—
So, silently, grimly, the steamer
Lurches ahead through the night.

A beacon-light far off,
Twinkling across the waves like a star!
But no star in the dark overhead!
The splash of waters at the prow, and the evil light
Of the death-fires flitting like will-o'-the-wisps beneath! And beyond
Silence and night!

I sit by the taffrail,
Alone in the dark and the blown cold mist and the spray,
Feeling myself swept on irresistibly,
Sunk in the night and the sea, and made one with their footfall-less onrush,
Letting myself be borne like a spar adrift
Helplessly into the night.

Without fear, without wish,
Insensate save of a dull, crushed ache in my heart,
Careless whither the steamer is going,

Conscious only as in a dream of the wet and the dark
And of a form that looms and fades indistinctly
Everywhere out of the night.

O love, how came I here?
Shall I wake at thy side and smile at my dream?
The dream that grips me so hard that I cannot wake nor stir!
O love! O my own love, found but to be lost!
My soul sends over the waters a wild inarticulate cry,
Like a gull's scream heard in the night.

The mist creeps closer. The beacon
Vanishes astern. The sea's monotonous noises
Lapse through the drizzle with a listless, subsiding cadence.
And thou, O love, and the sea throb on in my brain together,
While the steamer plunges along,
Butting its way through the night.

ISABEL

In her body's perfect sweet
Suppleness and languor meet,—
Arms that move like lapsing billows,
Breasts that Love would make his pillows,
Eyes where vision melts in bliss,
Lips that ripen to a kiss.

CONTEMPORARIES

"A barbered woman's man,"—yes, so
He seemed to me a twelvemonth since;
And so he may be—let it go—
Admit his flaws—we need not wince
To find our noblest not all great.
What of it? He is still the prince,
And we the pages of his state.

The world applauds his words; his fame
Is noised wherever knowledge be;
Even the trader hears his name,
As one far inland hears the sea;
The lady quotes him to the beau
Across a cup of Russian tea;
They know him and they do not know.

I know him. In the nascent years
Men's eyes shall see him as one crowned;
His voice shall gather in their ears
With each new age prophetic sound;
And you and I and all the rest,
Whose brows to-day are laurel-bound,
Shall be but plumes upon his crest.

A year ago this man was poor,—
This Alfred whom the nations praise;
He stood a beggar at my door
For one mere word to help him raise
From fainting limbs and shoulders bent
The burden of the weary days;
And I withheld it—and he went.

I knew him then, as I know now,
Our largest heart, our loftiest mind;
Yet for the curls upon his brow
And for his lisp, I could not find
The helping word, the cheering touch.
Ah, to be just, as well as kind,—
It costs so little and so much!

It seemed unmanly in my sight
That he, whose spirit was so strong
To lead the blind world to the light,
Should look so like the mincing throng
Who advertise the tailor's art.
It angered me—I did him wrong—
I grudged my groat and shut my heart.

I might have been the prophet's friend,
Helped him who is to help the world!
Now, when the striving is at end,
The reek-stained battle-banners furled,
And the age hears its muster-call,
Then I, because his hair was curled,
I shall have lost my chance—that's all.

THE TWO BOBBIES

Bobbie Burns and Bobbie Browning,
They're the boys I'd like to see.
Though I'm not the boy for Bobbie,

Bobbie is the boy for me!

Bobbie Browning was the good boy;
Turned the language inside out,
Wrote his plays and had his days,
Died—and held his peace, no doubt.

Poor North Bobbie was the bad boy,—
Bad, bad, bad, bad Bobbie Burns!
Loved and made the world his lover,
Kissed and barleycomed by turns.

London's dweller, child of wisdom,
Kept his counsel, took his toll;
Ayrshire's vagrant paid the piper,
Lost the game—God save his soul!

Bobbie Burns and Bobbie Browning,
What's the difference, you see?
Bob the lover, Bob the lawyer;
Bobbie is the boy for me!

A TOAST

Here's a health to thee, Roberts,
And here's a health to me;
And here's to all the pretty girls
From Denver to the sea!

Here's to mine and here's to thine!
Now's the time to clink it!
Here's a flagon of old wine,
And here are we to drink it.

Wine that maketh glad the heart
Of the bully boy!
Here's the toast that we love most,
"Love and song and joy!"

Song that is the flower of love,
And joy that is the fruit!
Here's the love of woman, lad,
And here's our love to boot!

You and I are far too wise
Not to fill our glasses.

Here's to me and here's to thee,
And here's to all the lasses!

THE KAVANAGH

A stone jug and a pewter mug,
And a table set for three!
A jug and a mug at every place,
And a biscuit or two with Brie!
Three stone jugs of Cruiskeen Lawn,
And a cheese like crusted foam!
The Kavanagh receives to-night!
McMurrough is at home!

We three and the barley-bree!
And a health to the one away,
Who drifts down careless Italy,
God's wanderer and estray!
For friends are more than Arno's store
Of garnered charm, and he
Were blither with us here the night
Than Titian bids him be.

Throw ope the window to the stars,
And let the warm night in!
Who knows what revelry in Mars
May rhyme with rouse akin?
Fill up and drain the loving cup
And leave no drop to waste!
The moon looks in to see what's up—
Begad, she'd like a taste!

What odds if Leinster's kingly roll
Be now an idle thing?
The world is his who takes his toll,
A vagrant or a king.
What though the crown be melted down,
And the heir a gypsy roam?
The Kavanagh receives to-night!
McMurrough is at home!

We three and the barley-bree!
And the moonlight on the floor!
Who were a man to do with less?
What emperor has more?
Three stone jugs of Cruiskeen Lawn,

And three stout hearts to drain
A slanter to the truth in the heart of youth
And the joy of the love of men.

A CAPTAIN OF THE PRESS-GANG

Shipmate, leave the ghostly shadows,
Where thy boon companions throng!
We will put to sea together
Through the twilight with a song.

Leering closer, rank and girding,
In this Black Port where we bide,
Reel a thousand flaring faces;
But escape is on the tide.

Let the tap-rooms of the city
Reek till the red dawn comes round.
There is better wine in plenty
On the cruise where we are bound.

I've aboard a hundred messmates
Better than these 'long-shore knaves.
There is wreckage on the shallows;
It's the open sea that saves.

Hark, lad, dost not hear it calling?
That's the voice thy father knew,
When he took the King's good cutlass
In his grip, and fought it through.

Who would palter at press-money
When he heard that sea-cry vast?
That's the call makes lords of lubbers,
When they ship before the mast.

Let thy cronies of the tavern
Keep their kisses bought with gold;
On the high seas there are regions
Where the heart is never old,

Where the great winds every morning
Sweep the sea-floor clean and white,
And upon the steel-blue arches
Burnish the great stars of night;

There the open hand will lose not,
Nor the loosened tongue betray.
Signed, and with our sailing orders,
We will clear before the day;

On the shining yards of heaven
See a wider dawn unfurled....
The eternal slaves of beauty
Are the masters of the world.

THE BUCCANEERS

Oh, not for us the easy mirth
Of men that never roam!
The crackling of the narrow hearth,
The cabined joys of home!
Keep your tame, regulated glee,
O pale protected State!
Our dwelling-place is on the sea,
Our joy the joy of Fate!

No long caresses give us ease,
No lazy languors warm,
We seize our mates as the sea-gulls seize,
And leave them to the storm.
But in the bridal halls of gloom
The couch is stern and strait;
For us the marriage rite of Doom,
The nuptial joy of Fate.

Wine for the weaklings of the town,
Their lucky toasts to drain!
Our skoal for them whose star goes down,
Our drink the drink of men!
No Bacchic ivy for our brows!
Like vikings, we await
The grim, ungarlanded carouse
We keep to-night with Fate.

Ho, gamesters of the pampered court!
What stakes are those at strife?
Your thousands are but paltry sport
To them that play for life.
You risk doubloons, and hold your breath.
Win groats, and wax elate;
But we throw loaded dice with Death,

And call the turn on Fate.

The kings of earth are crowned with care,
Their poets wail and sigh;
Our music is to do and dare,
Our empire is to die.
Against the storm we fling our glee
And shout, till Time abate
The exultation of the sea,
The fearful joy of Fate.

THE WAR-SONG OF GAMELBAR

Bowmen, shout for Gamelbar!
Winds, unthrottle the wolves of war!
Heave a breath
And dare a death
For the doom of Gamelbar!
Wealth for Gamel,
Wine for Gamel,
Crimson wine for Gamelbar!

CHORUS:—
Oh, sleep for a knave,
With his sins in the sod!
And death for the brave,
With his glory up to God!
And joy for the girl,
And ease for the churl!
But the great game of war
For our lord Gamelbar,
Gamelbar!

Spearmen, shout for Gamelbar,
With his Saxon thirty score!
Heave a sword
For our overlord,
Lord of warriors, Gamelbar!
Life for Gamel,
Love for Gamel,
Lady-loves for Gamelbar!

Horsemen, shout for Gamelbar!
Swim the ford and climb the scaur!
Heave a hand
For the maiden land,

The maiden land of Gamelbar!
Glory for Gamel,
Gold for Gamel,
Yellow gold for Gamelbar!

Armorers for Gamelbar,
Rivet and forge and fear no scar!
Heave a hammer
With anvil clamor,
To weld and brace for Gamelbar!
Ring for Gamel!
Rung for Gamel!
Ring-rung-ring for Gamelbar!

Yeomen, shout for Gamelbar,
And his battle-hand in war!
Heave his pennon;
Cheer his men on,
In the ranks of Gamelbar!
Strength for Gamel,
Song for Gamel,
One war-song for Gamelbar!

Roncliffe, shout for Gamelbar!
Menthorpe, Bryan, Castelfar!
Heave, Thorparch
Of the Waving Larch,
And Spofford's thane, for Gamelbar!
Blaise for Gamel,
Brame for Gamel,
Rougharlington for Gamelbar!

Maidens; strew for Gamelbar
Roses down his way to war!
Heave a handful,
Fill the land full
Of your gifts to Gamelbar!
Dream of Gamel,
Dance for Gamel,
Dance in the halls for Gamelbar!

Servitors, shout for Gamelbar!
Roast the ox and stick the boar!
Heave a bone
To gaunt Harone,
The great war-hound of Gamelbar!
Mead for Gamel,
Mirth for Gamel,

Mirth at the board for Gamelbar!

Trumpets, speak for Gamelbar!
Blare as ye never blared before!
Heave a bray
In the horns to-day,
The red war-horns of Gamelbar!
To-night for Gamel,
The North for Gamel,
With fires on the hills for Gamelbar!

Shout for Gamel, Gamelbar,
Till your throats can shout no more!
Heave a cry
As he rideth by,
Sons of Orm, for Gamelbar!
Folk for Gamel,
Fame for Gamel,
Years and fame for Gamelbar!

CHORUS:—
Oh, sleep for a knave
With his sins in the sod!
And death for the brave,
With his glory up to God!
And joy for the girl,
And ease for the churl!
But the great game of war
For our lord Gamelbar,
Gamelbar!

THE OUTLAW

Oh, let my lord laugh in his halls
When he the tale shall tell!
But woe to Jarlwell and its walls
When I shall laugh as well!
And he that laughs the last, lads,
Laughs well, laughs well!

He's lord of many a burg and farm
And mickle thralls and gold,
And I am but my own right arm,
My dwelling-place the wold.
But when we twain meet face to face,
He will hot laugh so bold.

The shame he chuckles as he shows
This time he need not tell;
I'll give his body to the crows,
And his black soul to Hell.
For he that laughs the last, lads,
Laughs well, laughs well!

THE KING'S SON

"Daughter, daughter, marry no man,
Though a king's son come to woo,
If he be not more than blessing or ban
To the secret soul of you."

"'Tis the King's son, indeed, I ween,
And he left me even but now,
And he shall make me a dazzling queen,
With a gold crown on my brow."

"And are you one that a golden crown,
Or the lust of a name can lure?
You had better wed with a country clown,
And keep your young heart pure."

"Mother, the King has sworn, and said
That his son shall wed but me;
And I must gang to the prince's bed,
Or a traitor I shall be."

"Oh, what care you for an old man's wrath?
Or what care you for a king?
I had rather you fled on an outlaw's path,
A rebel, a hunted thing."

"Mother, it is my father's will,
For the King has promised him fair
A goodly earldom of hollow and hill,
And a coronet to wear."

"Then woe is worth a father's name,
For it names your dourest foe!
I had rather you came the child of shame
Than to have you fathered so."

"Mother, I shall have gold enow,

Though love be never mine,
To buy all else that the world can show
Of good and fair and fine."

"Oh, what care you for a prince's gold,
Or the key of a kingdom's till?
I had rather see you a harlot bold
That sins of her own free will.

"For I have been wife for the stomach's sake,
And I know whereof I say;
A harlot is sold for a passing slake,
But a wife is sold for aye.

"Body and soul for a lifetime sell,
And the price of the sale shall be
That you shall be harlot and slave as well
Until Death set you free."

LAURANA'S SONG. FOR "A LADY OF VENICE"

Who'll have the crumpled pieces of a heart?
Let him take mine!
Who'll give his whole of passion for a part,
And call't divine?
Who'll have the soiled remainder of desire?
Who'll warm his fingers at a burnt-out fire?
Who'll drink the lees of love, and cast i' the mire
The nobler wine?

Let him come here, and kiss me on the mouth,
And have his will!
Love dead and dry as summer in the South
When winds are still
And all the leafage shrivels in the heat!
Let him come here and linger at my feet
Till he grow weary with the over-sweet,
And die, or kill.

LAUNA DEE

Weary, oh, so weary
With it all!
Sunny days or dreary—

How they pall!
Why should we be heroes,
Launa Dee,
Striving to no winning?
Let the world be Zero's!
As in the beginning
Let it be!

What good comes of toiling,
When all's done?
Frail green sprays for spoiling
Of the sun;
Laurel leaf or myrtle,
Love or fame—
Ah, what odds what spray, sweet?
Time, that makes life fertile,
Makes its blooms decay, sweet,
As they came.

Lie here with me dreaming,
Cheek to cheek,
Lithe limbs twined and gleaming,
Brown and sleek;
Like two serpents coiling
In their lair.
Where's the good of wreathing
Sprays for Time's despoiling?
Let me feel your breathing
In my hair.

You and I together—
Was it so?
In the August weather
Long ago!
Did we kiss and fellow,
Side by side,
Till the sunbeams quickened
From our stalks great yellow
Sunflowers, till we sickened
There and died?

Were we tigers creeping
Through the glade
Where our prey lay sleeping,
Unafraid,
In some Eastern jungle?
Better so.
I am sure the snarling

Beasts could never bungle
Life as men do, darling,
Who half know.

Ah, if all of life, love,
Were the living!
Just to cease from strife, love,
And from grieving;
Let the swift world pass us,
You and me,
Stilled from all aspiring,—
Sinai nor Parnassus
Longer worth desiring,
Launa Dee!

Just to live like lilies
In the lake!
Where no thought nor will is,
To mistake!
Just to lose the human
Eyes that weep!
Just to cease from seeming
Longer man and woman!
Just to reach the dreaming
And the sleep!

THE MENDICANTS

We are as mendicants who wait
Along the roadside in the sun.
Tatters of yesterday and shreds
Of morrow clothe us every one.

And some are dotards, who believe
And glory in the days of old;
While some are dreamers, harping still
Upon an unknown age of gold.

Hopeless or witless! Not one heeds,
As lavish Time comes down the way
And tosses in the suppliant hat
One great new-minted gold To-day.

Ungrateful heart and grudging thanks,
His beggar's wisdom only sees
Housing and bread and beer enough;

He knows no other things than these.

O foolish ones, put by your care!
Where wants are many, joys are few;
And at the wilding springs of peace,
God keeps an open house for you.

But that some Fortunatus' gift
Is lying there within his hand,
More costly than a pot of pearls,
His dulness does not understand.

And so his creature heart is filled;
His shrunken self goes starved away.
Let him wear brand-new garments still,
Who has a threadbare soul, I say.

But there be others, happier few,
The vagabondish sons of God,
Who know the by-ways and the flowers,
And care not how the world may plod.

They idle down the traffic lands,
And loiter through the woods with spring;
To them the glory of the earth
Is but to hear a bluebird sing.

They too receive each one his Day;
But their wise heart knows many things
Beyond the sating of desire,
Above the dignity of kings.

One I remember kept his coin,
And laughing flipped it in the air;
But when two strolling pipe-players
Came by, he tossed it to the pair.

Spendthrift of joy, his childish heart
Danced to their wild outlandish bars;
Then supperless he laid him down
That night, and slept beneath the stars.

THE MARCHING MORROWS

Now gird thee well for courage,
My knight of twenty year,

Against the marching morrows
That fill the world with fear!

The flowers fade before them;
The summer leaves the hill;
Their trumpets range the morning,
And those who hear grow still.

Like pillagers of harvest,
Their fame is far abroad,
As gray remorseless troopers
That plunder and maraud.

The dust is on their corselets;
Their marching fills the world;
With conquest after conquest
Their banners are unfurled.

They overthrow the battles
Of every lord of war,
From world-dominioned cities
Wipe out the names they bore.

Sohrab, Rameses, Roland,
Ramoth, Napoleon, Tyre,
And the Romeward Huns of Attila—
Alas, for their desire!

By April and by autumn
They perish in their pride,
And still they close and gather
Out of the mountain-side.

The tanned and tameless children
Of the wild elder earth,
With stature of the northlights,
They have the stars for girth.

There's not a hand to stay them,
Of all the hearts that brave;
No captain to undo them,
No cunning to off-stave.

Yet fear thou not! If haply
Thou be the kingly one,
They'll set thee in their vanguard
To lead them round the sun.

IN THE WORKSHOP

Once in the Workshop, ages ago,
The clay was wet and the fire was low.

And He who was bent on fashioning man
Moulded a shape from a clod,
And put the loyal heart therein;
While another stood watching by.

"What's that?" said Beelzebub.
"A lover," said God.
And Beelzebub frowned, for he knew that kind.

And then God fashioned a fellow shape
As lithe as a willow rod,
And gave it the merry roving eye
And the range of the open road.

"What's that?" said Beelzebub.
"A vagrant," said God.
And Beelzebub smiled, for he knew that kind.

And last of all God fashioned a form,
And gave it, what was odd,
The loyal heart and the roving eye;
And he whistled, light of care.

"What's that?" said Beelzebub.
"A poet," said God.
And Beelzebub frowned, for he did not know.

THE MOTE

Two shapes of august bearing, seraph tall,
Of indolent imperturbable regard,
Stood in the Tavern door to drink. As the first
Lifted his glass to let the warm light melt
In the slow bubbles of the wine, a sunbeam,
Red and broad as smouldering autumn, smote
Down through its mystery; and a single fleck,
The tiniest sun-mote settling through the air,
Fell on the grape-dark surface and there swam.

Gently the Drinker with fastidious care
Stretched hand to clear the speck away. "No, no!"—
His comrade stayed his arm. "Why," said the first,
"What would you have me do?" "Ah, let it float
A moment longer!" And the second smiled.
"Do you not know what that is?" "No, indeed."
"A mere dust-mote, a speck of soot, you think,
A plague-germ still unsatisfied. It is not.
That is the Earth. See, I will stretch my hand
Between it and the sun; the passing shadow
Gives its poor dwellers a glacial period.
Let it but stand an hour, it would dissolve,
Intangible as the color of the wine.
There, throw it away now! Lift it from the sweet
Enveloping flood it has enjoyed so well;"
(He smiled as only those who live can smile)
"Its time is done, its revelry complete,
Its being accomplished. Let us drink again."

IN THE HOUSE OF IDIEDAILY

Oh, but life went gayly, gayly,
In the house of Idiedaily!

There were always throats to sing
Down the river-banks with spring,

When the stir of heart's desire
Set the sapling's heart on fire.

Bobolincolns in the meadows,
Leisure in the purple shadows,

Till the poppies without number
Bowed their heads in crimson slumber,

And the twilight came to cover
Every unreluctant lover.

Not a night but some brown maiden
Bettered all the dusk she strayed in,

While the roses in her hair
Bankrupted oblivion there.

Oh, but life went gayly, gayly,

In the house of Idiedaily!

But this hostelry, The Barrow,
With its chambers, bare and narrow,

Mean, ill-windowed, damp, and wormy,
Where the silence makes you squirmy,

And the guests are never seen to,
Is a vile place, a mere lean-to,

Not a traveller speaks well of,
Even worse than I heard tell of,

Mouldy, ramshackle, and foul.
What a dwelling for a soul!

Oh, but life went gayly, gayly,
In the house of Idiedaily!

There the hearth was always warm,
From the slander of the storm.

There your comrade was your neighbor,
Living on to-morrow's labor.

And the board was always steaming,
Though Sir Ringlets might be dreaming.

Not a plate but scoffed at porridge,
Not a cup but floated borage.

There were always jugs of sherry
Waiting for the makers merry,

And the dark Burgundian wine
That would make a fool divine.

Oh, but life went gayly, gayly
In the house of Idiedaily!

RESIGNATION

When I am only fit to go to bed,
Or hobble out to sit within the sun,
Ring down the curtain, say the play is done,

And the last petals of the poppy shed!

I do not want to live when I am old,
I have no use for things I cannot love;
And when the day that I am talking of
(Which God forfend!) is come, it will be cold.

But if there is another place than this,
Where all the men will greet me as "Old Man,"
And all the women wrap me in a smile,
Where money is more useless than a kiss,
And good wine is not put beneath the ban,
I will go there and stay a little while.

COMRADES

Comrades, pour the wine to-night
For the parting is with dawn!
Oh, the clink of cups together,
With the daylight coming on!
Greet the morn
With a double horn,
When strong men drink together!

Comrades, gird your swords to-night,
For the battle is with dawn!
Oh, the clash of shields together,
With the triumph coming on!
Greet the foe,
And lay him low,
When strong men fight together!

Comrades, watch the tides to-night,
For the sailing is with dawn!
Oh, to face the spray together,
With the tempest coming on!
Greet the sea
With a shout of glee,
When strong men roam together!

Comrades, give a cheer to-night,
For the dying is with dawn!
Oh, to meet the stars together,
With the silence coming on!
Greet the end
As a friend a friend,

When strong men die together!

How many Canadians—how many even among the few who seek to keep themselves informed of the best in contemporary literature, who are ever on the alert for the new voices—realise, or even suspect, that this Northern land of theirs has produced a poet of whom it may be affirmed with confidence and assurance that he is of the great succession of English poets? Yet such—strange and unbelievable though it may seem—is in very truth the case, that poet being (to give him his full name) William Bliss Carman. Canada has full right to be proud of her poets, a small body though they are; but not only does Mr. Carman stand high and clear above them all—his place (and time cannot but confirm and justify the assertion) is among those men whose poetry is the shining glory of that great English literature which is our common heritage.

If any should ask why, if what has been just said is so, there has been—as must be admitted—no general recognition of the fact in the poet's home land, I would answer that there are various and plausible, if not good, reasons for it.

First of all, the poet, as thousands more of our young men of ambition and confidence have done, went early to the United States, and until recently, except for rare and brief visits to his old home down by the sea, has never returned to Canada—though for all that, I am able to state, on his own authority, he is still a Canadian citizen. Then all his books have had their original publication in the United States, and while a few of them have subsequently carried the imprints of Canadian publishers, none of these can be said ever to have made any special effort to push their sale. Another reason for the fact above mentioned is that Mr. Carman has always scorned to advertise himself, while his work has never been the subject of the log-rolling and booming which the work of many another poet has had—to his ultimate loss. A further reason is that he follows a rule of his own in preparing his books for publication. Most poets publish a volume of their work as soon as, through their industry and perseverance, they have material enough on hand to make publication desirable in their eyes. Not so with Mr. Carman, however, his rule being not to publish until he has done sufficient work of a certain general character or key to make a volume. As a result, you cannot fully know or estimate his work by one book, or two books, or even half a dozen; you must possess or be familiar with every one of the score and more volumes which contain his output of poetry before you can realise how great and how many-sided is his genius.

It is a common remark on the part of those who respond readily to the vigorous work of Kipling, or Masefield, even our own Service, that Bliss Carman's poetry has no relation to or concern with ordinary, everyday life. One would suppose that most persons who cared for poetry at all turned to it as a relief from or counter to the burdens and vexations of the daily round; but in any event, the remark referred to seems to me to indicate either the most casual acquaintance with Mr. Carman's work, or a complete misunderstanding and misapprehension of the meaning of it. I grant that you will find little or nothing in it all to remind you of the grim realities and vexing social problems of this modern existence of ours; but to say or to suggest that these things do not exist for Mr. Carman is to say or to suggest something which is the reverse of true. The truth is, he is aware of them as only one with the sensitive organism of a poet can be; but he does not feel that he has a call or mission to remedy them, and still less to sing of them. He therefore leaves the immediate problems of the day to those who choose, or are led, to occupy themselves therewith, and turns resolutely away to dwell upon those things which for him possess infinitely greater importance.

"What are they?" one who knows Mr. Carman only as, say, a lyrist of spring or as a singer of the delights of vagabondia probably will ask in some wonder. Well, the things which concern him above all, I would answer, are first, and naturally, the beauty and wonder of this world of ours, and next the mystery of the earthly pilgrimage of the human soul out of eternity and back into it again.

The poems in the present volume—which, by the way, can boast the high honor of being the very first regular Canadian edition of his work—will be evidence ample and conclusive to every reader, I am sure, of the place which

The perennial enchanted
Lovely world and all its lore

occupy in the heart and soul of Bliss Carman, as well as of the magical power with which he is able to convey the deep and unfailing satisfaction and delight which they possess for him. They, however, represent his latest period (he has had three well-defined periods), comprising selections from three of his last published volumes: The Rough Rider, Echoes from Vagabondia, and April Airs, together with a number of new poems, and do not show, except here and there and by hints and flashes, how great is his preoccupation with the problem of man's existence—

—the hidden import
Of man's eternal plight.

This is manifest most in certain of his earlier books, for in these he turns and returns to the greatest of all the problems of man almost constantly, probing, with consummate and almost unrivalled use of the art of expression, for the secret which surely, he clearly feels, lies hidden somewhere, to be discovered if one could but pierce deeply enough. Pick up Behind the Arras, and as you turn over page after page you cannot but observe how incessantly the poet's mind—like the minds of his two great masters, Browning and Whitman—works at this problem. In "Behind the Arras," the title poem; "In the Wings," "The Crimson House," "The Lodger," "Beyond the Gamut," "The Juggler"—yes, in every poem in the book—he takes up and handles the strange thing we know as, or call, life, turning it now this way, now that, in an effort to find out its meaning and purpose. He comes but little nearer success in this than do most of the rest of men, of course; but the magical and ever-fresh beauty of his expression, the haunting melody of his lines, the variety of his images and figures and the depth and range of his thought, put his searchings and ponderings in a class by themselves.

Lengthy quotation from Mr. Carman's books is not permitted here, and I must guide myself accordingly, though with reluctance, because I believe that in a study such as this the subject should be allowed to speak for himself as much as possible. In "Behind the Arras" the poet describes the passage from life to death as

A cadence dying down unto its source
In music's course,

and goes on to speak of death as

—the broken rhythm of thought and man,
The sweep and span
Of memory and hope
About the orbit where they still must grope
For wider scope,

To be through thousand springs restored, renewed,
With love imbrued,
With increments of will
Made strong, perceiving unattainment still
From each new skill.

Now follow some verses from "Behind the Gamut," to my mind the poet's greatest single achievement;

As fine sand spread on a disc of silver,
At some chord which bids the motes combine,
Heeding the hidden and reverberant impulse,
Shifts and dances into curve and line,

The round earth, too, haply, like a dust-mote,
Was set whirling her assigned sure way,
Round this little orb of her ecliptic
To some harmony she must obey.

And what of man?

Linked to all his half-accomplished fellows,
Through unfrontiered provinces to range—
Man is but the morning dream of nature,
Roused to some wild cadence weird and strange.

Here, now, are some verses from "Pulvis et Umbra," which is to be found in Mr. Carman's first book, Low Tide on Grand Pré, and in which the poet addresses a moth which a storm has blown into his window:

For man walks the world with mourning
Down to death and leaves no trace,
With the dust upon his forehead,
And the shadow on his face.

Pillared dust and fleeing shadow
As the roadside wind goes by,
And the fourscore years that vanish
In the twinkling of an eye.

"Pillared dust and fleeing shadow." Where in all our English literature will one find the life history of man summed up more briefly and, at the same time, more beautifully, than in that wonderful line? Now follows a companion verse to those just quoted, taken from "Lord of My Heart's Elation," which stands in the forefront of From the Green Book of the Bards. It may be remarked here that while the poet recurs again and again to some favorite thought or idea, it is never in the same words. His expression is always new and fresh, showing how deep and true is his inspiration. Again it is man who is pictured:

A fleet and shadowy column
Of dust and mountain rain,
To walk the earth a moment
And be dissolved again.

But while Mr. Carman's speculations upon life's meaning and the mystery of the future cannot but appeal to the thoughtful-minded, it is as an interpreter of nature that he makes his widest appeal. Bliss Carman, I must say here, and emphatically, is no mere landscape-painter; he never, or scarcely ever, paints a picture of nature for its own sake. He goes beyond the outward aspect of things and interprets or translates for us with less keen senses as only a poet whose feeling for nature is of the deepest and profoundest, who has gone to her whole-heartedly and been taken close to her warm bosom, can do. Is this not evident from these verses from "The Great Return"—originally called "The Pagan's Prayer," and for some inscrutable reason to be found only in the limited Collected Poems, issued in two stately volumes in 1905.

When I have lifted up my heart to thee,
Thou hast ever hearkened and drawn near,
And bowed thy shining face close over me,
Till I could hear thee as the hill-flowers hear.

When I have cried to thee in lonely need,
Being but a child of thine bereft and wrung,
Then all the rivers in the hills gave heed;
And the great hill-winds in thy holy tongue—

That ancient incommunicable speech—
The April stars and autumn sunsets know—
Soothed me and calmed with solace beyond reach
Of human ken, mysterious and low.

Who can read or listen to those moving lines without feeling that Mr. Carman is in very truth a poet of nature—nay, Nature's own poet? But how could he be other when, in "The Breath of the Reed" (From the Green Book of the Bards), he makes the appeal?

Make me thy priest, O Mother,
And prophet of thy mood,
With all the forest wonder
Enraptured and imbued.

As becomes such a poet, and particularly a poet whose birth-month is April, Mr. Carman sings much of the early spring. Again and again he takes up his woodland pipe, and lo! Pan himself and all his train troop joyously before us. Yet the singer's notes for all his singing never become wearied or strident; his airs are ever new and fresh; his latest songs are no less spontaneous and winning than were his first, written how many years ago, while at the same time they have gained in beauty and melody. What heart will not stir to the vibrant music of his immortal "Spring Song," which was originally published in the first Songs from Vagabondia, and the opening verses of which follow?

Make me over, mother April,
When the sap begins to stir!
When thy flowery hand delivers
All the mountain-prisoned rivers,
And thy great heart beats and quivers
To revive the days that were,
Make me over, mother April,
When the sap begins to stir!

Take my dust and all my dreaming,
Count my heart-beats one by one,
Send them where the winters perish;
Then some golden noon recherish
And restore them in the sun,
Flower and scent and dust and dreaming,
With their heart-beats every one!

That poem is sufficient in itself to prove that Bliss Carman has full right and title to be called Spring's own lyrist, though it may be remarked here that not all his spring poems are so unfeignedly joyous. Many of them indeed, have a touch, or more than a touch, of wistfulness, for the poet knows well that sorrow lurks under all joy, deep and well hidden though it may be.

Mr. Carman sings equally finely, though perhaps not so frequently, of summer and the other seasons; but as he has other claims upon our attention, I shall forbear to labor the fact, particularly as the following collection demonstrates it sufficiently. One of those other claims is as a writer of sea poetry. Few poets, it may be said, have pictured the majesty and the mystery, the beauty and the terror of the sea, better than he. His Ballads of Lost Haven is a veritable treasure-house for those whose spirits find kinship in wide expanses of moving waters. One of the best known poems in this volume is "The Gravedigger," which opens thus:

Oh, the shambling sea is a sexton old,
And well his work is done.
With an equal grave for lord and knave,
He buries them every one.

Then hoy and rip, with a rolling hip,
He makes for the nearest shore;
And God, who sent him a thousand ship,
Will send him a thousand more;
But some he'll save for a bleaching grave,
And shoulder them in to shore—
Shoulder them in, shoulder them in,
Shoulder them in to shore.

In "The City of the Sea" (Last Songs from Vagabondia) Mr. Carman speaks of the seabells sounding

The eternal cadence of sea sorrow
For Man's lot and immemorial wrong—
The lost strains that haunt the human dwelling
With the ghost of song.

Elsewhere he speaks of

The great sea, mystic and musical.

And here from another poem is a striking picture:

... the old sea
Seems to whimper and deplore
Mourning like a childless crone
With her sorrow left alone—
The eternal human cry
To the heedless passer-by.

I have said above that Mr. Carman has had three distinct periods, and intimated that the poems in the following collection are of his third period. The first period may be said to be represented by the Low Tide and Behind the Arras volumes, while the second is displayed in the three volumes of Songs from Vagabondia, which he published in association with his friend Richard Hovey. Bliss Carman was from the first too original and individual a poet to be directly influenced by anyone else; but there can be no doubt that his friendship with Hovey helped to turn him from over-preoccupation with mysteries which, for all their greatness, are not for man to solve, to an intenser realisation of the beauty and loveliness of the world about him and of the joys of human fellowship. The result is seen in such poems as "Spring Song," quoted in part above, and his perhaps equally well-known "The Joys of the Road," which appeared in the same volume with that poem, and a few verses from which follow:

Now the joys of the road are chiefly these:
A crimson touch on the hardwood trees;

A vagrant's morning wide and blue,
In early fall, when the wind walks, too;

A shadowy highway cool and brown,
Alluring up and enticing down

From rippled waters and dappled swamp,
From purple glory to scarlet pomp;

The outward eye, the quiet will,
And the striding heart from hill to hill.

Some of the finest of arman's work is contained in his elegiac or memorial poems, in which he commemorates Keats, Shelley, William Blake, Lincoln, Stevenson, and other men for whom he has a kindred feeling, and also friends whom he has loved and lost. Listen to these moving lines from "Non Omnis Moriar," written in memory of Gleeson White, and to be found in Last Songs from Vagabondia:

There is a part of me that knows,
Beneath incertitude and fear,
I shall not perish when I pass
Beyond mortality's frontier;

But greatly having joyed and grieved,
Greatly content, shall hear the sigh
Of the strange wind across the lone
Bright lands of taciturnity.

In patience therefore I await
My friend's unchanged benign regard,—
Some April when I too shall be
Spilt water from a broken shard.

In "The White Gull," written for the centenary of the birth of Shelley in 1892, and included in By the Aurelian Wall, he thus apostrophizes that clear and shining spirit:

O captain of the rebel host,
Lead forth and far!
Thy toiling troopers of the night
Press on the unavailing fight;
The sombre field is not yet lost,
With thee for star.

Thy lips have set the hail and haste
Of clarions free
To bugle down the wintry verge
Of time forever, where the surge
Thunders and trembles on a waste
And open sea.

In "A Seamark," a threnody for Robert Louis Stevenson, which appears in the same volume, the poet hails "R.L.S." (of whose tribe he may be said to be truly one) as

The master of the roving kind,

and goes on:

O all you hearts about the world
In whom the truant gypsy blood,
Under the frost of this pale time,
Sleeps like the daring sap and flood
That dreams of April and reprieve!
You whom the haunted vision drives,

Incredulous of home and ease.
Perfection's lovers all your lives!

You whom the wander-spirit loves
To lead by some forgotten clue
Forever vanishing beyond
Horizon brinks forever new;
Our restless loved adventurer,
On secret orders come to him,
Has slipped his cable, cleared the reef,
And melted on the white sea-rim.

"Perfection's lovers all your lives." Of these, it may be said without qualification, is Bliss Carman himself.

No summary of Mr. Carman's work, however cursory, would be worthy of the name if it omitted mention of his ventures in the realm of Greek myth. From the Book of Myths is made up of work of that sort, every poem in it being full of the beauty of phrase and melody of which Mr. Carman alone has the secret. The finest poems in the book, barring the opening one, "Overlord," are "Daphne," "The Dead Faun," "Hylas," and "At Phædra's Tomb," but I can do no more here than name them, for extracts would fail to reveal their full beauty. And beauty, after all is said, is the first and last thing with Mr. Carman. As he says himself somewhere:

The joy of the hand that hews for beauty
Is the dearest solace under the sun.

And again

The eternal slaves of beauty
Are the masters of the world.

A slave—a happy, willing slave—to beauty is the poet himself, and the world can never repay him for the message of beauty which he has brought it.

Kindred to From the Book of Myths, but much more important, is Sappho: One Hundred Lyrics, one of the most successful of the numerous attempts which have been made to recapture the poems by that high priestess of song which remain to us only in fragments. Mr. Carman, as Charles G. D. Roberts points out in an introduction to the volume, has made no attempt here at translation or paraphrasing; his venture has been "the most perilous and most alluring in the whole field of poetry"—that of imaginative and, at the same time, interpretive construction. Brief quotation again would fail to convey an adequate idea of the exquisiteness of the work, and all I can do, therefore, is to urge all lovers of real poetry to possess themselves of Sappho: One Hundred Lyrics, for it is literally a storehouse of lyric beauty.

I must not fail here to speak of From the Book of Valentines, which contains some lovely things, notably "At the Great Release." This is not only one of the finest of all Mr. Carman's poems, but it is also one of the finest poems of our time. It is a love poem, and no one possessing any real feeling for poetry can read it without experiencing that strange thrill of the spirit which only the highest form of poetry can communicate. "Morning and Evening," "In an Iris Meadow," and "A letter from Lesbos" must be also mentioned. In the last named poem, Sappho is represented as writing to Gorgo, and expresses herself in these moving words:

If the high gods in that triumphant time
Have calendared no day for thee to come
Light-hearted to this doorway as of old,
Unmoved I shall behold their pomps go by—
The painted seasons in their pageantry,
The silvery progressions of the moon,
And all their infinite ardors unsubdued,
Pass with the wind replenishing the earth

Incredulous forever I must live
And, once thy lover, without joy behold,
The gradual uncounted years go by,
Sharing the bitterness of all things made.

Mention must be now made of Songs of the Sea Children, which can be described only as a collection of the sweetest and tenderest love lyrics written in our time—

—the lyric songs
The earthborn children sing,
When wild-wood laughter throngs
The shy bird-throats of spring;
When there's not a joy of the heart
But flies like a flag unfurled,
And the swelling buds bring back
The April of the world.

So perfect and complete are these lyrics that it would be almost sacrilege to quote any of them unless entire. Listen however, to these verses:

The day is lost without thee,
The night has not a star.
Thy going is an empty room
Whose door is left ajar.

Depart: it is the footfall
Of twilight on the hills.
Return: and every rood of ground
Breaks into daffodils.

There are those who will have it that Bliss Carman has been away from Canada so long that he has ceased to be, in a real sense, a Canadian. Such assume rather than know, for a very little study of his work would show them that it is shot through and through with the poet's feeling for the land of his birth. Memories of his childhood and youthful years down by the sea are still fresh in Mr. Carman's mind, and inspire him again and again in his writing. "A Remembrance," at the beginning of the present collection, may be pointed to as a striking instance of this, but proof positive is the volume, Songs from a

Northern Garden, for it could have been written only by a Canadian, born and bred, one whose heart and soul thrill to the thought of Canada. I would single out from this volume for special mention as being "Canadian" in the fullest sense "In a Grand Pré Garden," "The Keeper's Silence," "At Home and Abroad," "Killoleet," and "Above the Gaspereau," but have no space to quote from them.

But Mr. Carman is not only a Canadian, he is also a Briton; and evidence of this is his Ode on the Coronation, written on the occasion of the crowning of King Edward VII in 1902. This poem—the very existence of which is hardly known among us—ought to be put in the hands of every child and youth who speaks the English tongue, for no other, I dare maintain—nothing by Kipling, or Newbolt, or any other of our so-called "Imperial singers"—expresses more truly and more movingly the deep feeling of love and reverence which the very thought of England evokes in every son of hers, even though it may never have been his to see her white cliffs rise or to tread her storied ground:

O England, little mother by the sleepless Northern tide,
Having bred so many nations to devotion, trust, and pride,
Very tenderly we turn
With welling hearts that yearn
Still to love you and defend you,—let the sons of men discern
Wherein your right and title, might and majesty, reside.

In concluding this, I greatly fear, lamentably inadequate study, I come to the collection which follows, and which, as intimated above, represents the work of Mr. Carman's latest period. I must say at once that, while I yield to no one in admiration for Low Tide and the other books of that period, or for the work of the second period, as represented by the Songs from Vagabondia volumes, I have no hesitation in declaring that I regard the poet's work of the past few years with even higher admiration. It may not possess the force and vigor of the work which preceded it; but anything seemingly missing in that respect is more than made up for me by increased beauty and clarity of expression. The mysticism—verging, or more than verging, at times on symbolism—which marked his earlier poems, and which hung, as it were, as a veil between them and the reader, has gone, and the poet's thought or theme now lies clearly before us as in a mirror. What—to take a verse from the following pages at random—could be more pellucid, more crystal clear in expression—what indeed, could come closer to that achieving of the impossible at which every real poet must aim—than this from "In Gold Lacquer".

Gold are the great trees overhead,
And gold the leaf-strewn grass,
As though a cloth of gold were spread
To let a seraph pass.
And where the pageant should go by,
Meadow and wood and stream,
The world is all of lacquered gold,
Expectant as a dream.

The poet, happily, has fully recovered from the serious illness which laid him low some two years ago, and which for a time caused his friends and admirers the gravest concern, and so we may look forward hopefully to seeing further volumes of verse come from the press to make certain his name and fame. But if, for any reason, this should not be—which the gods forfend!—Later Poems, I dare affirm, must and will be regarded as the fine flower and crowning achievement of the genius and art of Bliss Carman.

R. H. HATHAWAY.
Toronto, 1921.

Bliss Carman – A Short Biography

William Bliss Carman was born in Fredericton, in New Brunswick on April 15th 1861. 'Bliss' was his mother's maiden name. She was descended from Daniel Bliss of Concord, Massachusetts, who was the great-grandfather to Ralph Waldo Emerson.

Carman was educated at Fredericton Collegiate School. Here, under the influence of the headmaster George Robert Parkin, he gained an appreciation of classical literature and was introduced to the poetry of many of the Pre-Raphaelites especially Dante Gabriel Rossetti and Algernon Charles Swinburne.

From here he graduated to the University of New Brunswick, obtaining his B.A. there in 1881. As is common with so many writers his first published piece was for the University magazine and for Carman that was in 1879.

England now beckoned and he spent a year at Oxford and then the University of Edinburgh (1882–1883). He returned home to Canada to work on his M.A. which he obtained from the University of New Brunswick in 1884.

Tragically his father died in January, 1885, followed by his mother in February of the following year. Carman now enrolled in Harvard University for a year. There he met and was part of a literary circle that included the American poet Richard Hovey, who would become his close friend, and later collaborator, on the successful Vagabondia poetry series. Carman and Hovey were members of the "Visionists" circle along with Herbert Copeland and F. Holland Day, who would later form the Boston publishing firm Copeland & Day and, in turn, launch Vagabondia.

After Harvard Carman briefly returned to Canada, but was back in Boston by February of 1890 saying "Boston is one of the few places where my critical education and tastes could be of any use to me in earning money. New York and London are about the only other places." However, he was unable to find work in Boston but was more successful in New York becoming the literary editor of the semi-religious New York Independent. There he helped Canadian poets get published and introduced them to a wider readership than they could receive in Canada.

However, Carman and work as an editor were not destined for a long career together and he was dismissed in 1892. There followed short stays with Current Literature, Cosmopolitan, The Chap-Book, and The Atlantic Monthly. Whilst these appointments provided the basis for a career and an income he was not suited to their demands. From 1895 he would only work as a contributor to magazines and newspapers whilst he worked on his volumes of poetry.

Carman first published a book of poetry in 1893 with Low Tide on Grand Pré. He had written the title poem in the summer of 1886 and it had (whilst he was still at Harvard) been published in the spring of 1887 by Atlantic Monthly. Despite its critical acceptance there was no Canadian company prepared to publish the volume. When an American company did so it went bankrupt. Life was becoming difficult for the young poet.

The following year was decidedly better. His partnership with Richard Hovey had given birth to Songs of Vagabondia and it was published by their friends at Copeland & Day. It was an immediate success. The young men were delighted at such a reception. It quickly sold out and was re-printed a number of times. Although these re-prints were small (usually 500-1000 copies) they were frequent.

On the back of this success they would write a further three volumes, which in their turn were almost as successful. They quickly became the center of a cult following, especially among students who empathized with the poetry's anti-materialistic themes, its celebration of personal freedom, and its glorification of comradeship."

The success of Songs of Vagabondia prompted the Boston firm, Stone & Kimball, to reissue Low Tide on Grand Pré and to hire Carman as the editor of its literary journal, The Chapbook. This ceased after a year when the company relocated and Carman expressed his desire to remain in Boston.

In 1885 Carman brought out Behind the Arras, a somewhat more serious and philosophical work centered on the premise of a long meditation using the speaker's house and its many rooms as a symbol of life and the choices to be made. However, the idea and its execution did not quite meld.

Signficantly, in 1896, Carman met Mrs Mary Perry King, who rapidly became patron, adviser and sometime lover. She put money in his pocket, and food in his mouth and, when he struck bottom, often repaired his confidence as well as helping to sell the work. She also later became his writing collaborator on two verse dramas.

Mitchell Kennerley, Carman's roommate wrote that, "On the rare occasions they had intimate relations they always advised me of by leaving a bunch of violets — Mary favorite flower — on the pillow of my bed." If her husband, Dr. King, knew of this arrangement he seems not to have objected. He was a great supporter of Carman's career and seemingly his wife's complicated involvement with that.

In 1897 Carman published Ballad of Lost Haven, a collection of poetry about the sea. Its notable poems include the macabre sea shanty, The Gravedigger. The following year, 1898, came By the Aurelian Wall, the title poem itself was an elegy to John Keats and the book a collection of formal elegies.

In 1899 his publisher, Lamson, Wolffe was taken over by the Boston firm of Small, Maynard & Co., who had also acquired the rights to Low Tide on Grand Pré. The copyrights to of his books were now held by one publisher and, in lieu of earnings, Carman took what would ultimately be a disastrous financial stake in the company.

As the century turned Carman was hard at work on what would eventually be a five-volume set of poetry; "Pans Pipes". Pan, the goat-god, was traditionally associated with poetry and the coming together of the earthly and the divine. The five volumes were all published between 1902 – 1905.

The inspiration for this came from Mary who had persuaded Carman to write in both prose and poetry about the ideas of 'unitrinianism.' This drew on the theories of François-Alexandre-Nicolas-Chéri Delsarte and was defined as a strategy of mind-body-spirit harmonization aimed at undoing the physical, psychological, and spiritual damage caused by urban modernity. The definition may be rather woolly but for Carman it resulted in some very fine work across the five-volume series. This shared belief between Mary and Carman created a further bond but did isolate him from his circle of friends.

The excellence of a number of these poems did much to install Carman as the most noted of Canadian Poets and eventually their own Poet Laureate. Among the most often quoted and printed are "The Dead Faun" (from Volume I), "Lord of My Heart's Elation" (Volume II) and many of the erotic poems from Volume III.

In the middle of publication in 1903, Small, Maynard failed and with it went all the assets Carman had tied up in the company.

Carman immediately signed with another Boston publisher, L.C. Page, who would publish seven new books of Carman poetry in this hectic period up to 1905. They released a further three books based on Carman's Transcript columns, and a prose work on Unitrinianism, The Making of Personality, that he'd written with Mary King.

Carman now felt secure enough to pursue his 'dream project,' namely a deluxe edition of his collected poetry to 1903. Page acquired the distribution rights on the condition that the book be sold privately, by subscription. Unfortunately, the demand wasn't there and it failed. Carman was deeply disappointed and lost faith in Page. However, their grip on his copyrights was absolute and sadly no further collected editions were to be published during his lifetime.

By 1904 his income was restricted and the offer to be editor-in-chief of the 10-volume project, The World's Best Poetry, was eagerly accepted.

For Carman perhaps his best years as a poet were now behind him. From 1908 he lived near the Kings' New Canaan, Connecticut, estate, that he named "Sunshine", or in the summer in a cabin in the Catskills, which he called "Moonshine."

With Literary tastes now moving away from what he could provide his income further dwindled and his health started to deteriorate.

In 1912 Carman published the final work in the Vagabondia series. Richard Hovey had died in 1900 and so this last work was purely his. It has a distinct elegiac tone as if remembering the past works themselves.

Although Carman was not politically active he did campaign during the World War One, as a member of the Vigilantes, who supported the American entry into the titanic struggle on the Allied side.

By 1920, Carman was impoverished and recovering from a near-fatal attack of tuberculosis. He returned to Canada and began to undertake a series of publicly successful and somewhat lucrative reading tours, saying "there is nothing worth talking of in book sales compared with reading. Breathless attention, crowded halls, and a strange, profound enthusiasm such as I never guessed could be,' he reported to a friend. 'And good thrifty money too. Think of it! An entirely new life for me, and I am the most surprised person in Canada.'"

On October 28th, 1921 Carman was honored at a dinner held by the newly-formed Canadian Authors' Association, at the Ritz Carlton Hotel in Montreal, where he was crowned Canada's Poet Laureate with a wreath of maple leaves.

Carman is placed among the Confederation Poets, a group that included his cousin, Charles G.D. Roberts, Archibald Lampman, and Duncan Campbell Scott. Carman was perhaps the best and is credited with the widest recognition. However, whilst the others carefully supplemented their income with writing novels and works for the magazines, or even other careers, Carman only wrote poetry together with a small amount of writing on literary ideas, philosophy, and aesthetics.

He continued his reading tours, and by 1925 had finally secured a new Canadian publisher; McClelland & Stewart (Toronto), who issued a collection of selected earlier verse and would now became his main publisher. Although they benefited from Carman's increased popularity and his revered position in Canadian literature, his former publisher L.C. Page would not relinquish its copyrights to his earlier works.

In his last years, Carman was a member of the Halifax literary and social set, The Song Fishermen and in 1927 he edited The Oxford Book of American Verse.

William Bliss Carman died of a brain hemorrhage, at the age of 68, in New Canaan on the 8th June, 1929. He was cremated in New Canaan and his ashes interred at Forest Hill Cemetery, Fredericton, with a national memorial service held at the Anglican cathedral there.

It was only a quarter of a century later, on May 13th, 1954, that a scarlet maple tree was planted at his graveside, to honour his request in the 1892 poem "The Grave-Tree":

Let me have a scarlet maple
For the grave-tree at my head,
With the quiet sun behind it,
In the years when I am dead.

Bliss Carman – A Concise Bibliography

Poetry Collections
Low Tide on Grand Pre: A Book of Lyrics (1893)
Songs from Vagabondia (1894)
A Seamark: A Threnody for Robert Louis Stevenson (1895)
Behind the Arras: A Book of the Unseen (1895)
More Songs from Vagabondia (1896)
Ballads of Lost Haven: A Book of the Sea (1897)
By the Aurelian Wall: And Other Elegies (1898)
A Winter Holiday (1899)
Last Songs from Vagabondia (1901)
Ballads and Lyrics (1902)
Ode on the Coronation of King Edward (1902)
Pipes of Pan: From the Book of Myths (1902)
Pipes of Pan: From the Green Book of the Bards (1903)
Pipes of Pan: Songs of the Sea Children (1904)
Pipes of Pan: Songs from a Northern Garden (1904)
Pipes of Pan: From the Book of Valentines (1905)

Sappho: One Hundred Lyrics (1904)
Poems (1905)
The Rough Rider: And Other Poems (1909)
A Painter's Holiday, and Other Poems (1911)
Echoes from Vagabondia (1912)
April Airs: A Book of New England Lyrics (1916)
The Man of The Marne: And Other Poems (1918)
The Vengeance of Noel Brassard: A Tale of the Acadian Expulsion (1919)
Far Horizons (1925)
Later Poems (1926)
Sanctuary: Sunshine House Sonnets (1929)
Wild Garden (1929)
Bliss Carman's Poems (1931)

Drama
Bliss Carman & Mary Perry King. Daughters of Dawn: A Lyrical Pageant of a Series of Historical Scenes for Presentation with Music and Dancing (1913)
Bliss Carman & Mary Perry King. Earth Deities: And Other Rhythmic Masques (1914)

Prose Collections
The Kinship of Nature (1904)
The Poetry of Life (1905)
The Friendship of Art (1908)
The Making of Personality (1908)
Talks on Poetry and Life; Being a Series of Five Lectures Delivered Before the University of Toronto, December 1925 (Speech). transcribed by Blanche Hume. 1926.
Bliss Carman's Scrap-Book: A Table of Contents (Pierce, Lorne, editor) (1931)

Editor
The World's Best Poetry (10 volumes) (1904)
The Oxford Book of American Verse (U.S. editor) (1927)
Carman, Bliss; Pierce, Lorne, editors (1935). Our Canadian Literature: Representative Verse, English and French.

www.ingramcontent.com/pod-product-compliance
Lightning Source LLC
Chambersburg PA
CBHW060054050426
42448CB00011B/2453